The Ul Small Business Guide to Hiring Super-Stars

A New Formula Guaranteed to Find the Right People for Your Business

Jay Henderson

This book is dedicated first to my family – the most important people in the world! Thank you for your love and support. Also, to my clients all over the world. Thank you for your trust and allowing me to help you as you seek excellence in your business and life.

CONTENTS

ACKNOWLEDGMENTS

This book never would have happened without the help of many people. To my wonderful, inspiring, loving parents. Thank you, Mom and Dad, for *everything!* Thank you, Wayne Carpenter for all your teaching and help – which extends far beyond the book itself. You are an amazing person – a genius with a knowledge and expertise into the thought processes of the human mind that is likely unmatched in this world – you paid the price so you deserve it! Jennifer Absher, my personal assistant, for her journalistic acumen and clear-minded approach – which is why I hired her! Thank you to Darcy Juarez for her help in getting my thoughts out of my head and onto paper. Finally, to ALL my clients who have taught me so much as we've worked together on developing their businesses and teams. My appreciation to each of you!

WARNING: Hiring is a high-risk activity and when done wrong will likely cause a LOSS of the following: customers, revenue, profits, motivation, time, energy, happiness, and a sense of loss of your general well-being. You will also likely experience frustration, aggravation, potential migraines, a general malaise, and a possible desire for violence. Proceed with caution...

Jay Henderson

CHAPTER 1

What If Everything You Ever Learned About Hiring Employees Was Wrong?

When I ask small business owners what is the one thing that they dread the most, it's hiring good employees. At every conference where I speak, the question I am asked the most is… "How do I know who to hire?"

Well, you are about to discover the answer to that question, along with the answers to all your burning questions about finding, recruiting, attracting, interviewing, and choosing the *RIGHT* employees for you and your business. See, every business is different and, rightfully so,

3

deserves to have uniquely qualified super-star employees, and I'm here to show you how you can do that.

Wouldn't it be great if you could see inside a candidate's head – see what they are really like, how they think and make decisions, how they will really act on the job, not just what they say in a quick job interview?

What if I told you, you could?

You're about to discover what I have coined the Hiring MRI . Think about what happens when you twist a knee. Your doctor will examine you and ask some basic questions to rule out a few things (this would be equivalent to a phone interview.) He then goes into a deeper examination, possibly running a few basic mobility and strength tests (which would be equivalent to face-to-face interviews). And then if the basic tests warrant further review, he will order an MRI to be able to see what he can't see on the surface. This is the key to hiring super-stars that 99% of small business owners don't know how to do – and why should they?

Think about this for a second, that doctor has been trained to ask specific questions that will elicit a diagnosis. With that diagnosis, he can dig deeper with more specific questions, tests and examinations … but most of us, as small business owners, were never trained to ask specific questions when hiring or, more importantly, to understand what the answers that are given *really* mean. I am here to show you how you can do that…

The Hiring MRI formula has been responsible for placing tens of thousands of super-star employees and revolutionizing the way that small businesses hire – from law firms, to dental practices, and every business in between - and it isn't limited to small business. The Hiring MRI has been used by Red Robin Restaurants, Lance, HCCA, NASA, and more.

In addition to the sheer joy of finding super-star employees, small businesses using this formula for hiring have seen positive financial impacts. This is from a reduction in turnover and increased client satisfaction, and most importantly, they are happier and more productive business owners with the peace of mind that their business is thriving. This will allow them to focus on what they do best – productivity – all because they have found super-star employees.

Before we get started, let me introduce myself and tell you now why this might be the most important book you read this year.

My name is Jay Henderson, and I have spent the better part of the last 20 years helping entrepreneurs and small business owners hire super-stars in their respective businesses, drive greater success, and, more importantly, *block bad hires*. And I can tell you that, while it's not easy, it is something you can do and I'll show you how.

You see, a few years ago I applied for a job with a company that uses the principles of sports psychology to coach people to higher levels of performance in business. I had what turned out to be one of the most important job interviews of my life.

After the second interview, they had given me a simple exercise to complete. I couldn't imagine what they could possibly learn about me from this process, but I followed instructions and completed the exercise in about 15 minutes. I had filled out typical profiles before – but believe me, this was nothing like anything I had ever seen – there weren't even any questions.

During the next interview, the president of the company asked the most pointed, in-my-world discovery questions anyone had ever asked before. This man knew things about me no one could have or should have known.

I sat there stunned. How could he possibly know this? Fortunately, I got the job.

I've been passionate about how the mind works since I was a kid. I always wanted to understand why some people seem to win and some always seem to struggle.

Years later, looking back on it, I was lucky. My dad had given me Stephen R. Covey's now-famous "The 7 Habits of Highly Effective People" audio program. This was before the book was released and before he became a worldwide star.

Something in Covey's message really rang true with me. I listened to those tapes until I could almost recite them from memory. When the book came out a couple years later, I read it over and over as well.

I was hooked. I set a goal to work for Stephen Covey. It wasn't going to be easy. Covey's organization was based in Utah – I was living in North Carolina. I was young and had no experience in the training industry. But as you know, when goals are strong enough - answers come - and that's what happened for me.

I remember it like it was yesterday. I woke up the next morning, a beautiful North Carolina day, packed my car, and drove across the country to Utah. I didn't have a place to stay, and I didn't have a job - but I knew what I wanted. So I just did it.

About three months after I arrived in Provo, I was driving past a building I knew was part of the Covey Leadership Center. I had a clear impression to pull over, so that's exactly what I did.

I walked in the front door, and a woman asked, "Can I help you?" And the words just came out of my mouth. I answered, "I'm here to interview for a position." She asked if I'd seen the ad. I said, "No, I haven't seen the ad." I didn't even know they were interviewing. I was just following my impression. Amazingly, she interviewed and hired me right there on the spot.

Over the following years, I learned a ton from Stephen and his team, and I fell in love with an industry I have worked in for the past 25 years.

My experiences at Covey were great - but I decided to move to another company which led me to an opportunity to learn from another true genius, Wayne Carpenter. Wayne is the gentleman who refined, redesigned, and computerized the system we use today in companies of all sizes across America.

I have worked with large corporations, Fortune 500 companies, and the local mom-and-pop bakery. Every single business, regardless of its size, location, or personnel, struggles with hiring the 'right' people, but I believe that the impact this struggle has on the small business owner is magnified.

I wrote this book specifically for the entrepreneur and small business owner (the local dentist, attorney, doctor, financial planner, etc.) because I am a small business owner and entrepreneur and I know the impact bad hiring decisions have.

I've worked with hundreds of small business owners who all say, "I hate hiring. It's such a guessing game." Because they have been burned so many times by someone saying, "so-and-so is great! You should hire him." Or "I'm desperate to hire, because we can't function without someone, anyone."

Small businesses are impacted more by each team member's decisions and actions. There is less support by other team members who are often too busy to help. Every decision counts more. Costly mistakes are more difficult to overcome. Turnover impacts revenue, slows everything down, and even creates more turnover!

In working with hundreds of clients, I've seen firsthand the stress and frustration that high turnover and employee strain cause the small business owner. It can cause sleepless nights, constant worry about making payroll, and overall disappointment with their employees.

If you're like most small business owners and are currently struggling with:

- Under-performing employees
- A sense of (or a reality of) tension every time you try to motivate your employees to 'do their job'
- Employees with poor attitudes
- Employees who constantly show up late
- Feeling like you're working just to support your employees.
- Feeling like you are losing business, potential clients, customers, or patients
- Feeling like your employees are not committed to your cause or engaged
- Feeling like you have employees who are just working to get a paycheck

I'm here to show you that there is a better way! You'll learn what makes certain people super-stars, what makes others average employees, and why some people struggle in certain positions or situations.

I recently had a chance to work with Michael McCready of McCready, Garcia & Leet, a small law firm in Chicago.

Michael had mastered marketing, and his law firm was doing very well driving business. He decided that growing his team was the next critical element for his business. But he was so frustrated with the hiring process. In the past he would run a job ad and get hundreds of random resumes with everyone claiming to be the right person for the job. He invested a lot of valuable time and money into sorting through the hundreds of resumes and conducting countless interviews, only to feel at the end of the day like he was actually *guessing* about who to hire.

Once he hired someone, he still felt frustrated at how people either didn't perform, made a lot of expensive mistakes or, if they did perform, too often drove him nuts. He heard about my formula and decided to attend one of my hiring training events.

After learning the Hiring MRI formula, he was able to design his process pretty quickly and then applied the principles to his next hire. When he ran the new ad he designed from the formula, he only got 2 resumes.

First, he was concerned. "What went wrong?" he asked. Then he reviewed the resumes and learned that both looked perfect for what he was looking for. Could it be?

He was a bit concerned but also somewhat relieved when he called them for a first interview. After interviewing and completing the steps in the Hiring MRI formula, he had nailed it.

Sure enough, the two people who replied were perfect for the role and Michael was ecstatic. His "find a new attorney" project was done – he didn't have to spend useless hours weeding out resumes and interviewing people who wouldn't fit!

Here's what Michael had to say about the Hiring MRI formula...

"It's amazing how accurate Jay's system is, given the seemingly simple approach. I have paid much more attention to attracting, interviewing, hiring, and training the best people to get the most for my office staff since working with Jay.

Stop hiring and evaluating people on your gut instincts and rely on proven evaluative techniques in Jay's systems. You really don't know how amazing it is until you use it; then you will rely on it forever. Focus on what you know, in my case, being a lawyer, and rely on experts, such as Jay, for things which are beyond your expertise."

THAT is what this book is about.

I'll take you on a short journey similar to the one that Michael McCready went on so you can fully understand the power and principles of the Hiring MRI formula.

But first, you need to understand that **hiring for your small business is different**. The impact that each hire you make has on your business, your clients, and your reputation is magnified.

Think about that for a second. If a business has 3,000 employees, each employee (if weighted evenly) has .03% effect on each client. If there are 300 employees it's a .33% impact, and if there are only 3 employees, it's a 33% impact.

The decisions, actions, words that your employees make and use as a part of your small business have an enormous impact on your clients and customers. In larger businesses, there are natural layers of protection and large teams of people making decisions – in your business your employees may need to (and do) make critical decisions on behalf of your business every day.

Take, for instance, the receptionist or front desk person who is answering your phones. When a prospective client calls and asks questions specific about your business, - what type of answers she gives immediately impact whether or not that prospective client spends money in your business. That doesn't happen in larger businesses.

In small businesses, we are asking our employees to take on more and more roles. For many it isn't feasible to hire for every position you might need, so we combine roles together. Your front desk employee/receptionist may also be expected to be tech support.

You may have another employee who is in charge of your billing but at the same time is expected to greet clients as they come in, field phone calls, become an expert in your credit card processing… the list can go on.

Whereas, in a larger business, there is a specific person or even department who is responsible both internally and externally to solve those issues.

So you can see why hiring the *right people* in your small business becomes VERY important.

And when you get this right, it's life-changing! Because just one great hire can really change a small business. Just one. And then when you go on, adding more and more quality people, you will automatically build a strong culture. Performance and results will naturally increase. You will have less stress and fewer headaches. You will reach your goals faster. And your clients will be served better, be happier, and your profits will increase.

Part 1:

Why the Old Model of Hiring is Wrong

CHAPTER 2

Why the Game is Rigged Against You

By its very nature, the hiring process is stacked against us, and the process grows increasingly difficult every day.

We have to weed through the complexities of human nature. We are all geniuses at the subconscious level, and when a person sets a goal, especially an emotional goal, their subconscious genius is bound to achieve it.

Now, you might be wondering what that has to do with our job of hiring employees. It has everything to do with it!

Let's try to get into the mind-set of our job candidates – where they're coming from. They might be so unhappy at a current job that they see getting a new job as the solution that they have been praying for. One example, they could be a single mother with 4 kids at home and there only goal is to find a good-paying job that allows her to support her family.

The challenge is we don't know what their emotional motivation is and they usually won't tell us.

But all their drive and energy is focused on <u>their</u> goal. And at a subconscious level, their inner genius is going to be a great deal more engaged, because of the significant meaning and importance of this goal.

And when faced with this situation, suddenly all their hidden talent comes out in the interview. It's more than just a good first impression. They appear to be exactly what you are looking for.

But what happens when they accomplish their goal? Remember, their goal may have been just to *get* the job, not necessarily to *do* the job. Your goal was to get a long-term employee willing, capable, and able to do what you described in the job description (and interview) with a great attitude.

Once they have the job, their subconscious genius may shut off because they have accomplished the goal and their motivation and desire is no longer the same as it was during the interview. I have always said you can do anything you set your mind to for a short period of time, usually no more than 3 months (which just happens to put people past your 90-day probationary period, if you use one.) But what happens when you no longer 'need' to do something that you don't really want to do?

Think about the last time you tried to lose weight. Maybe it was for an upcoming vacation or it was your high school reunion. You decided that you could give up things you love for 3 months and do what you know you need to do to lose weight, but as soon as you pass that goal date, slowly but surely those bad habits start coming back – because you have 'accomplished your goal' by making it to your vacation or reunion.

When this happens, as the business owner, we often feel 'tricked.' As if the person we interviewed and the person currently working for us are two different people.

We end up with:

- Negativity
- Entitlement
- Lack of initiative
- Procrastination
- Resistance to change

- Pushing the boundaries
- Lack of respect
- Coming in 5-10 minutes late
- Leaving 5-10 minutes early
- Taking longer lunches
- Taking extra breaks
- Missing deadlines
- Work not being done
- Having to ask for things multiple times

So why does this happen? Most often it's because of what I call Hiring Insanity. You've probably heard you should *hire slow and fire fast* but most people tend to hire fast and fire slow.

The Hiring Insanity

Most people hire too fast when they have been left with a hole in their business, like when an employee leaves with only a 2-week notice (if we are lucky).

I recently had a client call me and say that he had an employee wait until 6 p.m. on a Friday night to send a text message to the office manager (not even to his boss, the owner) to say that he was giving his 2 weeks' notice AND was taking 2 weeks of vacation, and his key was on his desk. This is not an uncommon occurrence, and perhaps you can even top that story.

Finding and training a replacement in 2 weeks is virtually impossible. In fact, many reading this right now, may already be feeling the clock ticking on a 2 week notice. Don't worry, I have a plan for you! (it's revealed in Chapter 12)

CHAPTER 3

Why the Current Method of Hiring Doesn't Work for Small Businesses

As a business owner, finding great people is one of the most important things you can do and one of the most difficult. But the current process is flawed – and it's putting you at a significant disadvantage when hiring.

Most business owners wait until there is a hole in their business to start the process, most often when an employee has left or is leaving. They then create a job description based on what that employee was doing in their job. And they list out all the skills necessary to perform the job.

It might look something like this…

We are a national litigation support company with an office in downtown Chicago. The position we are seeking to fill is for deposition scheduling and client services. The duties entail answering the phones, scheduling depositions, assisting clients and working with court reporters. This is a full time position with benefits. Qualified candidates will have experience with receptionist duties, data entry, client services, scheduling and invoicing. Legal experience is not necessary but preferred.

They then wait for the resumes to come in, wade through the stack, and somewhat randomly determine who they will call to come in for an interview. And then they scour the Internet for the right questions to ask in an interview. Perhaps they have some others on the team interview the candidate.

Then they make their decision. Some might even elicit the help of a behavioral profile (sometimes referred to as a personality profile), to help them attempt to pick the best candidate.

This lack of a defined hiring system usually leads to ….

Hiring Too Quickly

When we are eager to fill a vacancy - or are being pressured by team members to just *fill a vacancy,* we're often willing to settle for less than the best. Sometimes the first person who walks through the door gets hired due to desperation.

Hiring on Gut Feelings

It is easy to rationalize, "I had a gut feeling that I should hire him, so I did." Sounds a lot like *guessing.* Appearances are deceiving and 9 times out of 10 you will be disappointed.

I believe in the value of using your gut instincts– just not as your only reason for hiring. If your gut is telling you <u>not</u> to hire someone, you should trust that. If your gut is telling you, you should hire someone, that's when you should slow down and look deeper.

If you are currently only using your gut to make decisions, it's an indication that you may not have a reliable system in place for this critical business task.

Hiring Based on Impeccable References

How many candidates aren't smart enough to provide you with references that will ensure them a glowing review?

Did you know that you can actually *BUY* glowing references? Career Excuse is a professional reference provider selling fake job references. They include a live operator acting as a supervisor's assistant for only $100! They will go as far as providing a virtual company website and email addresses for the fake company.

Not only that, but in today's litigious society, most employers are reluctant to reveal information about ex-employees – especially if it's negative. Many employers have adopted the name, rank, and serial number approach to reference requests. Under this approach they are only willing to give out the most basic information such as dates worked and positions held.

In fact, even if the employee was fired, the chances of that employer telling you that information (or the reasoning behind the firing) are very slim. So a 'good' reference from past employers really tells you very little.

Still, I think reference checks are important. You just need to know how to do them right.

Hiring Based Solely on the Interview

Most job applicants have attended a seminar or class on effective interviewing and are prepped for the interview. In fact, many colleges have this as a part of their curriculum.

Just Google "How do I ace an interview?" and you'll get over 9 million results all focused on helping the applicant achieve their goal of landing the job.

Then you'll truly ace your interview.

1. Identify Your "Hook" Most hiring managers interview a lot of people. ...
2. Know the Essence of the Job You're Applying For. ...
3. 3. ... ...
4. Know the Company. ...
5. Prepare a List of Follow-On Questions. ...
6. Practice, Practice, Practice. ...
7. Relax. ...
8. Stay Positive.

More items...

When I say that hiring gets harder every day, I am referring to this ...

How to Ace the 50 Most Common Job Interview Questions | Inc.com
www.inc.com/travis.../how-to-ace-the-50-most-common-interview-questions.html

About this result • Feedback

16 Psychological Tricks That Will Help You Ace A Job Interview
www.businessinsider.com/psychological-tricks-to-ace-job-interview-2... ▼ Business Insider ▼
Nov 11, 2015 - Schedule your interview around 10:30 a.m. on a Tuesday. Don't interview on the same
day as the strongest candidates. Match the color of your outfit to the image you want to project. Tailor
your answers to the interviewer's age. Hold your palms open or steeple your hands. Find something in
common with your interviewer.

How To Ace 10 Of The Most Common Interview Questions - Forbes
www.forbes.com/.../how-to-ace-10-of-the-most-common-interview-questions/ ▼ Forbes ▼
Jan 15, 2014 - But as it turns out, most companies will ask more common interview questions like
"What are your strengths?" and "What are your weaknesses?"—and it's important that you prepare well
for those, too. ... Glassdoor sifted through tens of thousands of interview reviews to find ...

20 years ago, if you wanted to prep for an interview and learn the interviewing questions, you had to leave your house, drive to the library or a bookstore, and invest in finding out the most asked interview questions and the best way to answer them. Now it takes less than a second on Google and we can have pages of sample questions.

interview question and answer

All   Videos   News   Images   Apps   More ▾   Search tools

About 17,100,000 results (0.49 seconds)

Answer Interview Questions - Audible.com
Ad www.audible.com/ ▾
Try Audible With A Free Audio Book! Download & Listen on iPhone/Android
Listen Anytime, Anyplace · Exchg Book You Don't Like · Sign Up w/ Amazon Account

31 Most Common Interview Questions and Answers | The Muse
https://www.themuse.com/.../how-to-answer-the-31-most-common-interview... ▾ TheMuse ▾
This is your interview question cheat sheet: Brilliant interview questions and answers you might be asked when going through the interview process.

Job Interview Questions and Answers - The Balance
www.thebalance.com › ... › Job Interviews › Job Interview Questions and Answers ▾
Review the most common job interview questions that employers ask, examples of the best answers for each question, and tips for how to respond.

10 Most Popular Interview Questions & Answers | Monster.com
www.monster.com/career-advice/article/top-10-interview-questions-prep ▾ Monster.com ▾
But many interview questions are to be expected. Study this list of popular and frequently asked interview questions and answers ahead of time so you'll be ...

Ten Tough Interview Questions and Ten Great Answers - CollegeGrad ...
https://collegegrad.com/...interview/ten-tough-interview-questions-and-ten-great-answ... ▾
Others are classic interview questions, such as "What is your greatest weakness?" Questions most people answer improperly. In this case, the standard textbook ...

Job Interview Questions and Answers - Job Searching - About.com
jobsearch.about.com › ... › Job Interviews › Job Interview Questions and Answers ▾
Review the most common job interview questions that employers ask, examples of the best answers for each question, and tips for how to respond.

And now that the Internet has made it so easy to get information, you are seeing articles and tips beyond just how to answer the interview questions but also what owners and hiring managers are looking for.

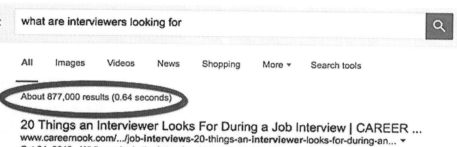

This makes the typical training on how to interview irrelevant.

However, it's important to consider that some applicants find interviews highly stressful; so nerve-wracking that they can't relax and let their real personality come through. They recognize that there's a lot on the line during this brief meeting.

Just like you wouldn't want to hire based on a single factor, you also don't want to eliminate a person too hastily because of a less-than-ideal interview demeanor.

Hiring Because of an Impressive Resume

I mentioned earlier that 53% of resumes contain false information (according the Society for Human Resource Management) and 51% lie about the length of stay at a past job, salary at a past job, and even their education. And again, thanks to the Internet, most job applicants think they know what we are looking, or asking, for:

- **Steady Employment, Few Gaps in Employment, and Longevity in Employment:** Leads to a propensity to exaggerate length of time at a position

- **Previous Salary:** Most believe that when asked this question it will lead to the starting salary offer at the new position – hence the propensity to increase previous salaries

- **Education Level:** Most job descriptions call for a college degree – hence the propensity to lie or omit.

- **Skills:** Most who read the resume are looking to match the skills that they are looking for with skills listed on the resume.

But how many times have you seen a resume perform on the job? Like a job reference, a good resume can be bought or created online.

Hiring based solely on the resume is like buying a car because you fell in love with the brochure. If you fail to test drive the car, look under the hood, and check that what the brochure states is the reality, you may end up with a lemon.

Hiring Because of a Recommendation

Many of us have hired someone who was recommended by a friend, family member, or colleague only to be stunned later when that employee didn't pan out. While your friend, family member, or colleague probably wants what's best for you - they may be operating under false assumptions.

Friends and family members typically have very little idea how someone performs in the workplace. A 'nice person' can be nice – but also absent-minded and lousy with details – not so great for your detail-oriented assistant position.

Relying on friends to send you a good employee is almost as reliable as your 'gut feeling.'

The Misgivings of Using Behavioral Profiles in Hiring

Many have recognized the need for something more than just a resume and interview to distinguish the best candidates and have invested in behavioral profiles for hiring. There are some famous ones out there that we've all heard of or had personal experiences with. They're interesting and they do reveal quite a bit about a candidate's current behavior.

But measuring behavior is like taking a digital photo of a person. You can tell a lot, but you're only guessing about what's happening on the inside.

And what these behavioral profiles don't do is assess your RISK and the exact problems you'll have to deal with when you hire someone. Some problems can't be managed! Also, they don't reveal other critical information about how the candidate will perform - which is the one thing that you really need to know!

When you can determine how a candidate makes decisions and the quality of their judgment, that is when you will be able to understand WHY they behave the way they do (even deeper than 'motivation') and can make important predictions about HOW they will perform in the future.

Unfortunately, using the same old hiring methods will continue to yield you the same old employee problems and will continue to cost you valuable time and money.

CHAPTER 4

What is the Real Cost of a Bad Hire?

There probably isn't a business owner alive who hasn't made a bad hire at some point. It's one reason why so many people who start businesses say they want to go as long as possible without hiring. But if we really want our businesses to grow and serve our community, hiring employees is a necessity. However, it shouldn't cost you an arm and a leg.

The challenging part of this is trying to put a true number on how much a bad hire costs *your* company! The numbers for this are all over the map. You may have heard figures like these:

- 10 times the employee's salary
- 5 times the employee's salary
- $7,000 to replace a salaried employee, $10,000 to replace a mid-level employee, and $40,000 to replace a senior executive (from HR.com)
- 30% of the individual's first-year potential earnings (US Department of Labor and Statistics)

There is no exact science to determine how much it costs you to hire. It is dependent on the role the bad hire plays in the company and the industry that you are in.

Here are the 6 areas that I look at when determining the cost of a bad hire.

Cost of Recruiting

This would include things like advertising, your time to review resumes, you and your teams' time to conduct interviews, drug screening and background checks (you are doing those, right?). I would also throw in the cost of recruiting firms or headhunters if you are using them.

Most people, when asked to place a cost on a bad hire, will only use the cost of recruiting because those are the only fixed costs that they can find expenses for. The next 5 are more subjective and harder for you to place a true value on.

Cost of Training

Once you have hired someone, you face a rampup time frame where they need to learn your business and your processes. Someone, most often you if the business is small, has to spend hours each day training the new hire on HOW to do everything in your business.

You must take time out of your productive schedule (time that would have been spent bringing in revenue for the company) to set up their email account, show them how to use your software, and teach them the ins and outs of the job that you are hoping they will perform well in.

Cost of Salary Plus Benefits

While salary is obviously a cost, most people do not spend enough time determining the true value of their benefits package.

This includes paid time off, holidays, sick time, medical insurance, bonuses, and 401k contributions and matches.

But then there are things like medical time, flexible hours, cell phone reimbursement, employee gifts, continuing education, expense allowances, dental/vision insurance, workmen's compensation, life insurance, access to health clubs, overtime/comp time, parking reimbursement, company meals that all are benefits of employment.

Cost of Integrating the Employee to Your Workplace

This includes things like a new computer, new office furniture, software or licenses, special equipment (like radios, pagers, phones, etc.), and office supplies.

Cost of Lost Opportunities

This is one of the big silent killers with a bad hire. Most business owners have no clue how much lost opportunity happens in their business daily. After all, how do you measure it? There are 2 types of lost opportunities as they relate to bad hires.

The lost opportunity in performance. You may have hired someone who performs at a level of 6 out of 10. So every day they were there, you lost 40% of potential performance. If this is in a sales or productivity role in your business, that's 40% of your potential revenue.

The second opportunity is in the lost opportunities to your business. The immeasurable. The business that came in, had an interaction with your bad hire, and then were never heard from again. And worse, the prospective clients who never even made it into your business after an interaction with your bad hire.

I was told about a receptionist who upon returning from a vacation picked up the phone and was overheard saying… *"Hold on a minute, this place is a mess. I have no idea where he is,* (turns out they were asking for the business owner). *Give me a minute. I will try to find him."*

I have another client, a dentist, who only learned through a secret shopper that when prospective patients called in asking for specific procedures and the schedule looked full or if they asked about having children seen, she answered that the doctor didn't do that or didn't see children and they should call Dr. so-and-so who was just down the street. And the doctor wondered why they couldn't attract new patients!

And then there are the customer service problems. There is no telling how many people have never come back to a business because they weren't treated at the level that they felt they deserved. How often do we throw a new hire into the fire of customer service? How often do we leave a bad hire in front of customers because it's better than having no one? Is it really?

The Cost of Turnover

Bad hires have a domino effect on your business.

I worked with a client who had built up his law practice over 3 years and had 3 super-star employees. Revenue had increased rapidly each year. They felt ecstatic about the work they were doing and really jelled as a team. As the work grew, he decided to bring on a fourth employee, and within just a couple of months, two of his previous employees quit and he lost half of his revenue as clients pulled out. That one bad hire almost cost him $300,000 in business.

In many companies, it's not that obvious. It might appear to be 'bad luck' that you had 2 employees receive opportunities they just couldn't turn down. Doubtful they will ever tell you the real reason they are leaving is due to their awful coworker.

So you can see why and how the costs of a bad hire can add up quickly and why it's so important to slow down during the hiring process to ensure that you have the *right* candidate for the job and for your company.

A bad hire can be particularly stressful to your super-star employees and to you. You are forced to spend all your time and energy trying to save the hire you made while the work doubles for the super-stars and they start to resent the situation. One of the best things you can do with super-star employees is to surround them with other high-performing people. This will help you spend your time preparing for success rather than repairing failures!

CHAPTER 5

Why is it so Difficult to Find 'Good' People?

The number one question I get is "How do I find good people?" And I wish that I could tell you they all reside in Raleigh, NC or that you will know them because they have a degree from this college or they have specific skills, but that's just not true.

The good news is that many high-performing, super-star employees are sitting nearby as you eat dinner at your favorite restaurant or jogging past you at the local park. The truth is most are not out there looking for a job so you just have to know how to find and attract them. Natural-born super-stars are rarely combing the want ads looking for a job. So, the first thing to do is continually maintain a hiring mind-set, keeping an eye out for good people wherever you go.

The second way to find good talent is to recognize the raw skills that will become good talent and then seek out those who are talented but are being overlooked.

Often we find great talent who just don't have the 'right' resume and have been overlooked by others. For instance, they might not have a college degree and, therefore, automatically get ruled out of certain jobs.

Or maybe they don't possess the exact skills that you *thought* were required (but in reality aren't) and they are passed over for those jobs.

Yet, they have the talent, intelligence, and capabilities ready to bring to the table.

I was working with a law client who decided to take a chance on hiring a girl with no high school or college degree, who had a rough life, but when she was put through the Hiring MRI formula had a strong probability of being a high-preforming employee who was overlooked by everyone because she didn't have the right degree. Well,

2 years later both the employee and the employer couldn't be happier.

And we could be doing this to ourselves with the job descriptions we write. There is a pool of people who read your job description, and think to themselves, I am not qualified for that job and never apply. They self-reject and you never have the opportunity to even have a conversation with them.

Maybe you list that they need to have a medical background – because you are a medical practice. But you are hiring for a front desk person, not a medical practitioner. So do they really have to have a medical background? How many good people are passed over because they have never worked in a medical practice before?

Many times a high-performing employee won't fit an exact mold. They won't possess every skill you are looking for, they won't have all the degrees and certifications that you are looking for, but they may have the key traits you are looking for – the ones you need. **And that is the key!**

And you must be careful, because what looks like a super-star because of high performance in a previous company may not turn out to be a high performer in your business.

This has been proven repeatedly and is one of the most frustrating things when hiring.

High-performing employees are more about the right focus, judgment and attitude, the fit with your culture, your current team, and your communication style than it is about the hard skills that they possess. Though the skills are important too.

When you start implementing the Hiring MRI formula, you will likely find that you are hiring people you never would have interviewed and not hiring people you would have hired before.

You see, finding high performers is not just about finding talent. Everyone has talent, but you need to find the people who have both talent and can *access* their talent. **Access is key**.

Today we live in a sort of celebrity-obsessed, visually based culture because of television. Sadly, many are often swayed into believing that looking good and being articulate equals talent and performance. But of course, nothing could be farther from the truth.

We need a reliable way of discerning between what 'looks' like talent and what 'is' talent. Consider the following graph about Talent vs. Access.

Talent vs. Access

They "Look Great"

The Fooler

Strong Talent
Weak Access
Weak Performance

The Super Star

Strong Talent
Strong Access
Strong Performance

They Have Weak
Access to Talent

They Have Strong
Access to Talent

The Flop

Toxic thinking patterns you
couldn't see
Somehow sneak in
Biggest problem/cost

The Sleeper

Less Visible Talent
Strong Access
Strong Performance

They "Don't Look
Great"

Quadrant I is The 'Fooler.' These candidates are tricky because in every way they seem like stars. They probably *look* like performers. They interview well. They are enthusiastic. Their resume is aligned with your needs. Their references check out. They may have done this job successfully in your industry.

They may have the talent, but the problem is they have little access to their talent and their performance will disappoint. They will become a waste of your time and resources. The faster we can identify the 'Fooler,' the better off you will be.

Quadrant II is The 'Superstar.' These are those with talent and access to their talent. These are the candidates who will look 'good,' will fit into your environment, and whose talents will create the greatest results for your business. They will not only save you money over the course of business - but will produce far above their cost to you.

Quadrant III is The 'Flop.' The Flops are your biggest problem and will cost you the most money. They have lower-than-desired talent and poor access to the talent they have. Somehow they slip into your business too easily and at great expense: in profitability, time, resources, stress, and your performance-based culture. They often have toxic thinking patterns that severely impact your environment, making mistakes and even causing your great employees to leave because of the culture they create.

Quadrant IV is The 'Sleeper.' We LOVE the Sleepers! These candidates may not 'look' so talented or seem to be a fit, but because they are found to have great access to their talent, they will totally surprise you with consistent performance and very good results. They are too often over-looked for your business, but they will drive the results you seek.

Your goal is to avoid those in Quadrants I and III and hire those in Quadrants II and IV. They have Real Talent and will perform for YOU.

Defining access over talent in someone is a unique science. The discovery is in *what* you measure and *how* you measure it.

Jay Henderson

Part 2:

How to Use the Hiring MRI Formula to Hire YOUR Super-Stars

Jay Henderson

CHAPTER 6

What Is the *Right* Way to Hire Super-Stars?

The reason why everything we have talked about until now doesn't solve your hiring headaches is because they are all just pieces of a larger puzzle. Under the current model, we don't know *WHY* the different pieces of the puzzle work. or don't work. This puts us at a huge disadvantage when hiring and means everything that we are doing is really only as good as the toss of a coin.

The current model of hiring may tell you if someone CAN do the job they are interviewing for (based on past experiences), but it doesn't answer two very important questions that will determine if they will be a super-star employee in _your_ business...

1. WILL they do the job?

2. Will they do the job FOR YOU in your unique business?

The new model for hiring is developed specifically to determine HOW potential employees will perform in YOUR business and with your culture.

"Will they do the job?" and "Will they do the job for you and in your culture?" are two questions that aren't on most small business owners' radar when hiring.

So what does this mean?

First, '**Will they do the job?**' This is big and I'd guess virtually no one asks themselves this question about their job candidates. It's tough… how would you even answer this question?

Research shows that there are a lot of people who can do a job, but there's no promise they will; perhaps they won't. Meaning, they might be able to and say they can, but in the end, they just won't.

Second, '**Will they do the job for you?**' We've proven that just because they *CAN* do the job and have shown it in the past does not guarantee that they *CAN* and *WILL* do that job *FOR YOU* and your unique business. There are too many variables that affect performance.

Why is this so important? The one attribute that most people base their hiring decision on is enthusiasm. This is backed up in study after study conducted by The Society for Human Resource Management.

Paying greater attention to this idea of people succeeding in a specific role *FOR YOU* will help tremendously in the hiring process. There's the idea of a person fitting the role you're hiring for. But then, does the candidate fit with the person who will be their boss? Do they fit within the systems in *your* business? There's even the issue of do *you* fit for *them*?

Here are 5 more pieces of the puzzle to consider:

1. There are basic reasons someone will not do the job – becoming Foolers or Flops. Maybe their drive and energy is not engaged. Gallup Poll research indicates that 71% of people are not engaged at work. Perhaps thy aren't getting along with their team or boss. Or maybe they're underwater and their skills aren't enough. Some people even go so far as to sabotage projects or clients.

Often in small businesses, employees are close

enough to the business that they get an idea of the boss' income and jealousy may set in. Or their own ideas about money come into play and they stop collecting fees from patients or clients.

They may not perform well because they have extra jobs you don't know about. Perhaps their lifestyle is such that they don't have enough energy to perform. Maybe they don't have any passion for the job you're asking them to do for you. Or maybe they just don't like the long commute.

2. Most people have no idea what their own performance is like. They're probably not even aware of their own performance inconsistencies. You can bet that the same will be true of your job candidates. They even fool themselves.

    I call this the "American Idol" effect. You've possibly seen this show where would-be singing super-stars go on television to try out for stardom… and are completely awful singers! Then, to make matters worse, they are stunned, legitimately shocked, when told how bad they are and turned away.

    This is why even world-class athletes, the best of the best, have coaches. They know they need that extra set of eyes to help them see the *reality* in their golf swing, or tennis stroke, or surgery skills, or trial preparation, etc.

3. Intentions are very powerful. Some people set a goal to get a job… but, believe it or not, don't have a goal to do the job effectively. All their drive and energy is engaged when answering your ad and interviewing with you. But when they get the job, that same level of energy and commitment isn't quite there. Although this is not typically done consciously, it happens every day.

   Therefore, while a candidate's resume and maybe even reference checks look good, they *won't* perform because they didn't quite have a goal to perform on the job.

4. Let's dive even deeper. By nature, some people are 'individualistic.' This means they do things their own way. While many people value *systems* to help run their lives or businesses, Individualists don't naturally value them. Along those lines they may think of themselves as team players, but in reality, it doesn't usually enter their attention because as Individualists, they're possibly not even aware of team dynamics.

There are levels to this bias ranging from the covert Individualist down to the rebel non-conformist (do-it-my-way person), all the way to seething rebellion (chip on the shoulder, sub-culture hippies). Finally, there's your delinquent, who is naturally driven to always break the rules.

So when considering the question, "Will they do the job?" the answer is maybe. With them (the Individualist), it comes down to their willingness – literally. In other words, will they do the job is not so much due to performance capacity, but their bias as an Individualist could cause them *not to* perform.

5. Other people are naturally 'Inner Directed' thinkers. I could fill a book about this type of thinking.

    Briefly, most people think more clearly about others and the world going on outside than they do about themselves. So they have an easier time understanding and fitting themselves into the world around them. Whereas, Inner Directed thinkers see and appreciate the 'self' more clearly than the 'world.' Their ability to think about themselves has developed beyond their ability to think about the world and other people. So when they find an environment/job that fits *them*, they can be super-stars.

However, when their thinking, alternatives, and ideas do not fit or are not accepted, they become susceptible to anxiety and frustration. I'm not describing the typical frustrations that result from a difficult conversation or, say, differences in opinion. It happens when the world outside them is not aligning with *their* own view and way of thinking. When this misalignment happens, it generates tremendous stress for them. They may make *mistakes* on purpose, *refuse* to take action, or become *irrational,* literally get up and *leave* meetings just to avoid the stress.

One illustration of how an inner-directed person differs is to use the square peg and round hole analogy. Most of the population can easily fit themselves into the world around them. But Inner Directed people cannot. It's not as if it's their desire – they just don't see it.

This can lead to inconsistent performance results both in themselves and with their team. So, if your environment does not fit them, even though they can do the job… they may not do the job for you.

In the old model of hiring – and in interviewing all we can see (based on answers) are the actions candidates have taken in the past (and we then expect that they will take the same actions in the future.)

We all expect results from our employees. But where do those results come from?

What Drives Results?

We all know that results come from actions, but no action is taken until a <u>decision</u> is made. That is why knowing HOW a candidate makes decisions and the quality of their judgment (remember the Talent vs. Access graph in Chapter 5) is the key to understanding *will* they do the job and will they do the job in your culture.

To make a decision, the mind takes 4 critical steps.

The 4 Decision-Making Steps

When we make decisions, we all go through the same basic process. First, you *perceive* information based on your perspective of the world (you allow some in, and you filter some out). Second, you *analyze* that information. Third, you make a *decision*, Fourth, you *act* on that decision.

But what does this have to do with hiring a super-star employee? **EVERYTHING!**

The key to hiring and performance is in knowing how your candidate goes through those 4 decision-making steps – both the *way* and how *well* they go through them.

In other words, your capacity to organize your thinking and emotions to make decisions is based on your talent for:

- Seeing and filtering what is happening around you, and in yourself
- Building concepts and ideas by focusing on what is important to you
- Translating your ideas and expectations into decisions

For example, have you ever looked through a window that was so clear it seemed as if it wasn't even there? It's like there's nothing blocking your ability to see. When everything is crystal clear, it's easy to make better decisions. You can easily connect the dots; you 'get' it. Good judgment = Good decisions.

Compare the clarity of that window to one that is covered in dirt and mud. It would be a struggle to see through it. How can you make great decisions if you don't see things clearly? Impaired judgment = Poor decisions.

It's not about intelligence. Everyone sees the world and themselves with their *own* filter of focus – some clear, some unclear.

Your ability to make judgments is natural, similar to musical talent and ability. Everyone has certain inborn skills or aptitudes. Some individuals have an ear for musical notes, while others can be taught to recognize the notes.

In the same way, some individuals have better developed natural talent for making better decisions. These individuals have a clearer idea of what is important, can see things which others miss, are very creative problem solvers, make decisions that always seem to be on target, and are sensitive to the needs and concerns of others. The ability to make good decisions is what I call Real Talent.

Real Talent

We should be looking for employees with the ability to access what I call their *Real Talent* which is the true marker of whether someone has the talent you want in your organization to succeed. This is the ability to access their talent for the role you are giving them. We identify Real Talent by *objectively* measuring their focus, judgment, and clarity.

Their *Real Talent* will tell us if they CAN do the job, if they WILL do the job and if they will do the job FOR YOU in your company's culture.

So how do you identify potential employees who have this *Real Talent?* By using the Hiring MRI formula (of course).

CHAPTER 7

What is the Hiring MRI Formula?

The Hiring MRI formula involves preparation to find and attract your super-stars. We approach this like we approach marketing our products or services in our business – we can't just expect that people will show up ready to buy from us. It is our job in marketing to share the knowledge, awareness, and reasons that people will want our products and services.

The same is true of our employees. We must share the knowledge, awareness, and reasons why they will want to work for us. After all, if you approach hiring just to get 'anybody,' that's exactly who you will attract.

As we have seen, super-stars aren't always hiding in plain sight and they won't be attracted to chaos and uncertainty. Super-stars are attracted to companies that know what they are looking for and where they are going.

So to get better hiring results, take the time to consider exactly what you want before you start looking for your super-star.

Be aware... while your website should sell potential candidates on your company and job opportunities, when you get someone into your office, never hype or sell a person into your company or the available position. Some people are in transition in life and don't know what they want to do, what they want to be, or where they'll fit in best. They are susceptible to your influence, and that could come back to bite you!

The first thing you will want to do is create your super-star job profile.

The Super-Star Job Profile

Before you begin you'll need to get in the right frame of mind and be strict about your needs. Your mind-set is critical to this process so write down these words:

"I will not lower my standards and hire subpar candidates!"

By making it difficult for a new person to be hired, you weed out marginal candidates.

The following process will help you do just that so you can get the best possible people on your team. But this requires discipline on your part. As the saying goes, you can lead a horse to water, but you can't make it drink ... well, that's exactly what I'm doing here. I'm leading you right up to the water with these steps. But you do actually need to do them. Take your time and do this stuff right, and it will pay off in a big way.

With this profile, you will want to write down the talents, strengths, skills, and competencies that you want for each position you are looking to fill. Without knowing this, you can't know when you have found the right person.

You will also want to focus on the performance you want, not just the position. There is a very big difference and this is the first step in finding and hiring super-stars. You are looking to find the desires and attitudes that are successful in your company and for this role. You are also looking for WHY people have been successful in the past so you can find that in the future.

Here are the 4 areas you should focus on.

1. Who are we? What is our business? (Just as you can't
    attract clients and customers without being clear on
    what you do, you must do the same for attracting
    your employees.)
    *What is your company culture? What plans do you have
    for growth/expansion? What makes your company
    different? Why would someone want to work for you?*

2. Who is the person I need?
    a. What does it take to succeed in this role?
        *For example, I might be a dentist who does a lot of
        charity and service work and I dedicate and give my
        time and resources, 2x a year for charity cases, and I
        am looking to hire someone who values service as a
        high priority in their life. (This has nothing to do with
        their skills to the job — but someone who values
        service, will succeed, and fit in the culture of this
        practice.)*

        *I might be looking for a personal assistant ...
        Organized*

        - *I travel a lot, so there is a lot of scheduling and
          booking that will need to be done.*
        - *I am an entrepreneur with 100 different things
          going on, and I need someone who can keep my*

schedule (and my life) organized and make sure that I make all my obligations (both work and personal).

b. What are the barriers to success in this role?
   Need to have your own car — I need someone who can organize my personal and professional life, which means I may need you to run errands for me, and you will need to have your own car with insurance.

   You will need to thrive in an ever-changing entrepreneurial environment. I can't promise that what we do today we will do tomorrow, so if you need consistency in your work, this might not be for you.

c. What are the attitudes that we would <u>want</u> them to possess?

d. What are the attitudes that they would <u>need</u> to have?

e. What would others in the company look for from this person?

f. What has made someone successful in this position in the past?

3. Describe your expected outcomes in detail.

    a.   What makes someone who fills this role a success?

    b.   Will this role change if the company changes?

    c.   List the results/accomplishments you expect to see....in the first 60 days, the first 9 months, and the first 18 months.

4. Determine specialized knowledge/skills/abilities that are required for success.
    a.   How will they go about doing their work? (For example, do they need to be organized or a self-starter?)

    b.   Create your list of "Needs" and "Wants" for this role.

Once you have determined what this role requires, you can create a checklist for each interview.

On your checklist, you will list all the wants, needs, skills, attitudes, behaviors, abilities, knowledge, talents, etc., that will apply to this role.

This will give you the ability to score each candidate based on your criteria (your first metric in your Hiring MRI formula).

To download a copy of my Super-Star Hiring Profile go to:

www.TryRealTalent.com

Okay. Now that you have your super-star hiring profile complete, you are ready to start creating your super-star magnet.

The Super-star Magnet

Otherwise known as your ad or job listing. This becomes very easy to write, once you have your super-star profile because you can now write directly to your ideal candidate.

Your ad should include:

1. Job Title (with a clear explanation).
2. Short blurb about your company and why it's a great place to have a career *(Remember super-stars aren't just looking for a job; they are looking for a place they can possibly grow and make a difference.*
3. Core responsibilities and expectations.

4. Skills required *(Make this a list of 'needs' as opposed to just 'wants.' You can train somebody with the right attitude to do a lot of skills, but you can't take the skills and turn them into a better attitude.)*

5. Possible salary range *(This can automatically screen applicants for you. You have to decide if you want that or not.)*

6. Growth potential.

7. Specific directions on how to apply – including 'hoops,' 'tasks,' or 'tests' to complete.

Back in Chapter 3 – I showed you an example of a typical job listing

where they focus on the duties of the job and mention nothing about the *person* who they are looking for.

We are a national litigation support company with an office in downtown Chicago. The position we are seeking to fill is for deposition scheduling and client services. The duties entail answering the phones, scheduling depositions, assisting clients and working with court reporters. This is a full-time position with benefits. Qualified candidates will have experience with receptionist duties, data entry, client services, scheduling and invoicing. Legal experience is not necessary but preferred.

Compare that to the one on the next page…

Looking for an experienced Part-time Executive Assistant for a Consulting Firm (Manhattan)

Are you a self-starter, comfortable working independently with little supervision and minimal direction?

Is "organized" your middle name because you love systems, planning, and time management?

Are you able to multi-task and prioritize projects while meeting deadlines?

Are you able to communicate professionally and effectively with people of all backgrounds, both written and verbal?

Can you anticipate the needs of others because you pay attention to even the smallest details?

Are you positive, creative, flexible, smart – with experience using Word, Excel, PowerPoint, Outlook, QuickBooks and online research?

Do you have high ethical and quality standards and are you able to exercise discretion and confidentiality?

If you answered yes to the above questions, then we can't wait to talk to you!

This prestigious consulting firm with an international client base is looking for an experienced and motivated Executive Assistant to support the principal and manage the office functions.

Position is permanent part-time. Competitive salary based on experience.

Qualified applicants should email a cover letter and resume to the address listed above with the subject line "Organized is my middle name."

As small business owners, our time is valuable, so there is one more thing that I throw into job postings. I give applicants a hoop or two to jump through. This will allow you to immediately weed out those that can't or won't follow instructions – after all, if they can't follow the directions when applying for the job, why would we think they will do it while on the job?

You can do this by simply adding a few lines in your job listing to include things like:

- The name of the person to reply to *If you don't get a response personalized to this person – it should tell you something).*
- You can ask them to "perform" for you. Give them something to do that shows their initiative, personality, and attention to detail.
- You can ask applicants to state why they are the best fit to join your team.
- You can ask them to include their list of references.
- You can ask them to provide their availability for a telephone interview.

Here is another sample job posting. This ad does a good job of speaking to the candidate. It also gives a specific way to respond to the ad, making it easier to weed out resumes from people who don't follow directions well.

Full-Time Front Medical Office Position in Metro City

Have you always wanted to work in a small office where you are an integral part of the TEAM? Do you love working with people and helping make their experience the best one possible? Have you ever visited Disneyworld and thought, "I wish every place was like this"? If you answered yes to all three questions, this job may be for you.

We are a busy but small medical practice in the northern area of Metro City. This position is one of the most important in the office. It involves daily and constant work with our patients, making them feel welcome and comfortable. A love of all people is a must for this job! You will also be the primary person to handle the phones and schedule patient appointments. You will greet them when they arrive as well. Positive energy in everything you do is a must.

It is also important that you are comfortable using a computer. This position involves data entry and word-processing on a daily basis. If using a computer scares you, this isn't the right fit.

If you're a person who starts your day with a smile and ends it with a bigger smile, definitely consider applying for this position. To apply, email us... (make sure you spell well and write English correctly) ...the subject line must read: "I'm your new Front Office TEAM member"

> In your email, tell me why you are the best fit to join our TEAM. Let your personality shine through on this. Also, be sure to send your resume as an attachment to your email.
>
> No phone calls…email only.

Here is a sample recruiting ad. This ad does a good job of describing the job requirements and responsibilities. It also asks for a specific response.

> **Great Summer Job for College Student Interested in Marketing (Metropolis)**
>
> If you are home from college (or will be soon) AND you are studying marketing or business AND you haven't been able to find the summer job of your dreams, this may be the perfect opportunity for you ...
>
> We are a small law firm that is one of the country's leaders in effective marketing for attorneys. We rock the Internet. We are looking for someone to help us over the summer by helping us produce hundreds of instructional videos, blogs, articles, and podcasts and blasting them all over the Internet. (Sounds daunting, doesn't it? This will be a blast!)
>
> What's really cool about this job is that once you learn the systems that we use, you can easily either work part time all year long (from your dorm room) or develop your own side

business helping professionals (lawyers, dentists, chiropractors, etc.) market. This will be a great job for someone who is at least a little bit Internet savvy and who is a self-starter--meaning that while you will spend part of your time in our office working with us to develop a strategy and produce content, you will spend the bulk of your time working on your own laptop, at your place or the library... in other words, you must be hardworking, diligent, and trustworthy. (If you are the type of person who, when you respond to this ad, has to ask us "Now what was the ad I was responding to?" then we don't want you. If you can't keep an appointment, we don't want you. If you think society owes you something, we don't want you!)

We know there are good hardworking students out there-the kind that make parents proud. You were the kid whose parents didn't have to log onto "Blackboard" when you were in high school to see what your homework was!!!

We pay $10/hr. and we expect you'll be able to work about 30-40 hours a week. It would be a really good idea to check out the OurBusiness.com site before you apply, and you might want to Google us, "Attorney John Doe," to get a feel for what we are already doing marketing wise.

Experience with a handheld video camera, some basic video editing and knowledge of PowerPoint is pretty essential.... You don't need to be an expert in Our Business... we'll learn its full capabilities together. Basically, we are looking for someone who is smart, can follow directions and wants to have a cool fun job this summer.

To apply, email us... (make sure you spell well, write English correctly--and all those other things that the career center at your school is telling you.)

The subject line must read: "Let's Rock Our Business"

In your email tell us that you are willing to work this summer job for $10/hr. and if you have done some things along these lines before, make sure to tell us about them!

We will check YOU out on the Internet so if what we find is a whole bunch of pictures of you getting drunk or otherwise acting inappropriately, keep on applying to flip hamburgers.

No phone calls - email only. We are ready to hire this week!

You will want to run your ad in as many different places as possible to cast a wide net. Remember the "sleepers" won't be as easy to recognize, and the "super-stars" may not be actively searching for a job. Don't forget to include your listing on your own website, on your LinkedIn profile, and Facebook (You never know who will be watching.)

I have a client who found a super-star employee in a most unusual way who was not actively searching for a job. He had set up 'Google news alerts' to notify him anytime the name of his favorite influential leader popped up online. So when my client's job posting went live and mentioned this influential person in the ad, the super-star saw the ad and decided to apply.

With these 2 steps, we should have laid the groundwork to find and attract high-performing candidates for our job. Our next step will be to determine which candidates get an interview from all the resumes received.

CHAPTER 8

I Have Resumes Coming In. Now What Do I Do?

The hoops you added to your job posting will start the process of weeding out marginal candidates. Now we will want to implement a process for sorting resumes.

Put them in two piles, one for resumes with a cover letter and one for those without. Then find the cover letters that are customized to you – this shows the applicant is serious. They have looked at your business and put forth the effort to show *why* they want to work for you.

Here are the things I look for when sorting through a pile of resumes:

- Look closely at the employment dates and the number of companies each person has worked for over the last 5-10 years. Are they stable or a job-hopper?
- Review for background or work experience that closely matches what you are looking for. If you are looking for a leader – have they shown leadership in the past?
- Look at the details of the submission. What did they name the file? Is it simply "Resume" or rather "John Doe – Great Employee?"
- Do you see any of their personality in the cover letter, or does it appear to be copied and pasted from a generic sample?
- Note grammar and spelling skills, did they take time to spell-check?
- Does the cover letter explain any gaps in the resume? Do they sound positive or are they complaining about positions or employers?
- Google the candidates you might like to interview! Enter their name in the search engine with other identifiers, such as their city and see what comes up. Do they have an online presence? If so, you can learn a lot about your potential employee. Check Facebook, Twitter, or LinkedIn.

Interviewing for Super-Stars

Once you have narrowed down the resumes, you are ready to bring in your top choices for the interview.

There are hundreds and hundreds of questions you can ask a candidate. Many are useful, but the best strategy is to prepare and make sure you are asking questions that will draw upon their attitudes, skills, and ability to access their talents for the role you are looking to fill.

Remember, the purpose of the interview is:

- To determine *can* and *will* the applicant do the job *for you*
- To determine *why* they are applying specifically for this position and with you
- To determine whether they are a *fit* for you, your team, and your company
- To determine if *you* are a fit for the candidate

Always remember, this interview is not about you. Most bosses, because they were never trained in how to interview powerfully or are not prepared, end up talking about themselves in interviews. They spend the time telling the applicant about their company and how great it is to work there and what they want from this position instead of talking about the candidate and learning whether the applicant has *Real Talent*.

So let's talk about the mechanics of the questions you should be asking and your approach to interviewing. So many of the questions out there are superficial (and Google has provided the applicant with the answers that they should provide.)

Those questions don't help you see or understand a candidate's *Real Talent* (i.e., how they will perform on the job). In the next chapter we go in depth into how to do this, with specific examples and questions for you to use as you interview for super-stars.

The first interview should be a 10-minute phone call. Don't waste your time sitting down with everyone. On this call, you are listening for attitude and tone of voice. You can ask basic questions such as:

- What are they looking for in the advertised position?
- Are they currently employed? Why are they considering leaving?
- Why did they leave their last job?
- What is their perfect position?
- How would they describe themselves?

- What would their last boss say about their work performance?
- What qualifications do they have that will help them succeed in the tasks you're looking for?
- How well can they work under pressure? Give an example?
- What can they tell you about your business/industry?

Then you can take the best of these candidates and invite each in for a 30 - 45-minute face-to-face interview.

From here, I would invite several people to interview the candidate. You will want to provide each interviewer with a scoring page that you create, based on your super-star profile and job posting (from Chapter 7). This will allow each person interviewing candidates to compare them against the same criteria — yours!

To download the template of the Interviewing Score Sheet I use, go to: www.TryRealTalent.com

When interviewing, I like to follow the rule of three:

1. Interview at least 3 people before you hire one.
2. Interview an applicant at least 3 times.
3. Have 3 different people in your business interview them.

In the next chapter, we will look at how to structure the face-to-face interview and the questions that will allow you to truly understand their ability to access the talents needed to succeed in your business.

CHAPTER 9

Interview Questions that *REALLY* Work

Your number one job is to climb inside the mind of the applicant to find out if they CAN do the job, if they WILL do the job, and if they will do the job for YOU. To do this, we have to break away from the norm. You must knock the applicant off their game so they are not giving you canned answers they think you want to hear.

You want to put your best foot forward, asking appropriate but unpredictable questions. Your job is to remove all emotion and dig to gather as much information about the candidate as possible, to reveal their *Real Talent.*

To do this, you want to make the candidate feel comfortable – it will take a few questions and a little time for them to settle in and reveal their true self. You can start with the 'standard questions' like things you see on their resume, why they want the job, why they believe they are a good fit for the job, how they think their competencies and skills fit the job.

When I am interviewing for an entrepreneurial enterprise or a small business, I look for 4 things that can tell a lot about a candidate:

1. Did they grow up in small business or with an entrepreneurial parent?
2. Did they grow up on a farm?
3. Did they participate in extracurricular activities?
4. Have they worked in restaurants or the service industry?

After covering the 'basics,' I will start chit-chatting about their high school, college years – asking about what their favorite subjects were, what did they participate in with the goal of getting them to talk freely about their life. I have two goals at this point.

1. To loosen up the tense interview situation by getting the candidate to talk about themselves,

especially when they don't think they are being judged.

2. To dig deeper into WHY they did the things that they did – WHY they excelled at the things they excelled at. WHY they gravitated towards certain things, WHY they didn't continue with other things.

Let's look at how you might interview someone who played sports growing up...

I would ask questions like:

- Were you involved in sports or other extracurricular activities? (You want to know what activities or sports specifically, including whether they were team sports or individual sports.)
- What position did you play?
- What do you like about team sports?
- What don't you like about team sports?
- What do you like about individual sports?
- What don't you like about individual sports?
- How long did you play in that sport?
- What did you like best about your sport?

- How did you juggle practice, timing, and school responsibilities all at the same time?

I am looking for things like...

- **Commitment Level:** Were they up at 4:00 a.m. daily for swim practice? Did they succeed in multiple sports or with sports and school combined? Did they lead their team or earn awards?

- **Level of Engagement**: Did they enjoy being a part of a team? Were they happy taking direction from the coach? What did and didn't they like about their coach? How did they handle losing?

- **Level of Loyalty:** Did they stick with the sport for an extended period of time? Did they continue at the collegiate level?

You are looking for happy, committed, loyal people. So it only makes sense that if that is the pattern of behavior in their past, it is a decent indicator of the behavior that they will have in the future.

If they came from a family who owned a small business, I might ask things like:

- What did you do in the business?
- What kind of business was it?
- How long did your family own the business?
- How long did you work in the business?
- What skills did you learn?
- What do you think having parents who owned a business did for you growing up?
- Have you ever thought of owning your own business?

And if they have worked in restaurants in the past, I like to ask things like…

- How long did you work at there?
- What did you like best about waiting tables? What else?
- What did you like least? What else?
- Which shift was your favorite? Why?

When you feel they are comfortable with the interview process so far and you've built up a good rapport, you will want to start digging deeper with follow up questions, looking for the real answer, not just the trite practiced reply the candidate believes you want to hear.

The idea is that you drill down on their answers to your questions, using their own language, to get to the truth or real reasons for why they answer as they do.

I call this process **Four-Level Deep Questioning**. It's simply a matter of making sure you go deeper than asking just one question, getting their first response and moving on. This will allow you to get past the superficial rehearsed answer.

For example, you might ask the candidate, "What do you think you will like most about this job?"

Say the candidate replies, "I like the flexibility you described in the job posting."

So that would lead you to ask (first deeper level question) "What is it about flexibility that appeals to you?"

Perhaps the candidate would then reply, "I like that if my schedule changes and if I need to come in later, I would be able to adjust my time to come in, but stay later that day so that I get the same amount of hours in."

The second follow-up question on this issue might be "Okay. Do you expect that your schedule will change often?

A third-level question might be "Is there a potential schedule conflict that we should be aware of?"

In this example, **Four-Level Deep Questioning** has allowed you to dig deeper, clarify, and spot potential issues a candidate may not have revealed if you simply took their first answer. You simply turn their answers into another question to follow up until you think you've hit the real answer.

When interviewing, I also like to talk about problems they might have solved in their past and dive deeper into examples. Because the more details the candidate knows about a problem, how it was solved, etc., the more confident you can be that they had an impact on that problem and solution, rather than simply having watched from the outside as someone else fixed a problem.

One of my favorite ways to do that is to ask, "Will you tell me what *your* thinking was or how you thought through this problem?" I really want to understand their pattern of thinking. "First I did this, then I did this, then this to resolve the problem." This is a glimpse into how they make decisions.

Follow up with "What was it like when you first learned about this problem?" and "What did you start thinking about?"

Through all of these questions, we are trying to find out how they thought through these issues. Did they 'see' the problem? How did they know it was a problem? Why did they decide to correct it the way they did? We want to do our best to learn how they think. Also, you're looking for how they acted in the past to determine patterns of behavior that can potentially predict their future behavior.

Next we'll dive into what you're looking for when hiring for certain types of roles.

CHAPTER 10

Hiring for Typical Positions - What to Look for

While there is no universal super-star profile for all positions, there are some definite performance indicators that super-star employees have in certain job categories and things to look for.

Reception/Customer Service Positions:

- Great Attitude
- Empathy – Warm
- Connection
- Organized

- Cool Under Pressure
- Appealing
- Nice Tone of Voice
- Appropriate
- Professional
- Patient
- Good Judgment

This role requires some training but also relies heavily on attitude and people skills. Training can be taught on the job, but remember, this is typically the person who creates the first impression for your business. Way too many people underestimate the importance of this customer service role. Judgment is critical. You don't want someone who is indifferent to people, who won't relate or connect well, and who may feel the client or customer is interrupting their work.

Sales Positions:

- Great Attitude
- Urgency
- Intuitive
- Ego Driven
- Goal Oriented
- Motivated
- Competitive
- Results Oriented
- Love Selling

So in sales, if a person has a strong drive matched with lots of empathy, can read a client, and they *want* to sell, then chances are good that they can succeed – UNLESS they overanalyze, are blocked by perfectionistic tendencies, aren't quick on their feet, can't be flexible and move with the client, can't 'read' the client, have poor self-esteem, lack confidence… and more.

Which illustrates how someone might look good on paper, but if we haven't looked under the hood, we won't know.

Medical/Dental Assistant:

- Great Attitude
- Intuitive
- Quick on their Feet
- Good Problem-Solving
- Organized
- Good Listening and Communication Skills
- Detail Oriented
- Patient
- Good Judgment

This role requires certain technical skills and training but also relies heavily on attitude and people skills. If the empathy and caring is not there for the patients or the assistant is overly rigid and controlling, it will not go well for the patients, the doctor, and ultimately the practice will suffer. Yet, no one may ever know the cause.

Paralegal Positions:

- Urgency
- Detail orientated
- Focused
- Self-starter
- Process oriented
- Results oriented
- Good judgment

The Common Denominator

You'll notice that having good judgment is a bedrock need for super-star employees. When a person has poor judgment, they won't make great decisions for you and your business and problems will abound.

The bottom line is, some problems can't be managed, and poor judgment is the biggest issue to watch out for.

How will you know when someone has poor judgment? This is difficult to identify, though there are some obvious clues: missing appointments, being late, not following through. To find poor judgment you need to look for a lot of poor decisions from their recent past.

Unfortunately, just because we don't see poor judgment in an interview process doesn't mean they have good judgment.

The biggest challenge in looking at behavior as the indicator of good judgment is that good judgment is more about how people think and make decisions; it's the precursor to behavior.

This is where you'll find the judgment capacity. You've got to look more deeply for WHY they made the good decisions they made. Just the shift in paradigm from focusing on behavior to focusing on the *thinking* that causes that behavior can make a huge impact for you.

I advise people to look for extremes in decisions and behaviors. Things like: poor problem-solving, overly emotional, impulsive, or irrational. People who have difficulty prioritizing, poor common sense, or are slow thinking, dogmatic, and rigid. These are difficult to identify with the naked eye, but if you believe you're seeing these things, dig deeper.

Remember, the reason everyone focuses on behavior so much is because we can see it. So we rely on it. There we are, back to the visual television era, believing everything we see.

Everything to this point is critical and necessary. These steps will help you have a better pool of candidates to choose from. However, without the last piece of the Hiring MRI formula, you'll still be guessing. If you want to *know* exactly what is going on in your applicant's mind, you can only get it with the Hiring MRI Performance Assessment.

The Hiring MRI Performance Assessment

This is the shortcut to get inside your applicant's mind. Rather than personality or behavior, it reveals <u>how they think and make decisions</u> and provides you with the key insights to their thinking and decision-making capabilities, PLUS it will give you the exact questions to ask each candidate to dig deeper.

This will help you identify the most important elements for each candidate – their *Real Talent* and your RISK before you ever hire them.

CHAPTER 11

The Hiring MRI Performance Assessment – Don't Risk Hiring Without It

So what exactly is the Hiring MRI Performance Assessment?

We have talked a lot about needing to determine not only can a candidate do the job, but WILL they do the job and will they do the job for us. Which is another way of asking will they perform. Our entire Hiring MRI formula has been created to figure that out.

You might ask, is there any way that we can measure performance? And the answer is yes! It's the last step in the Hiring MRI formula, and while there is a cost involved in running this test, it just might be the best investment you make in your business.

Earlier we talked about how the human mind works and how people perceive data, associate that data with things that they've seen before, analyze that data, and then make a decision. **Then they take action (behavior).**

Behavior is where other assessments start – measuring the action phase, *after* the decision has been made. Some do a good job by going backwards trying to understand why that behavior is the way it is. I'm all for you getting as much information about your candidate as you can. But it is still not a 100% reliable, direct measure of the **decision-making process, which is what accurately and reliably predicts performance**.

Because after all, making great decisions is the best tool we have in business. The ability to make great decisions consistently or to make better, more accurate, and faster decisions is key.

With the Hiring MRI Performance Assessment, we have the ability to see into the mind of your candidates just like a medical MRI – allowing us to see what can't be seen on the surface.

We can see things like:

- Judgment capacity
- Ability to see potential problems
- Ability to plan and organize
- Level of attention to detail
- Common sense
- Leadership competencies
- Management competencies
- Customer service competencies
- Sales competencies
- Project management competencies
- Professional and personal competencies
- If their strong sense of individualistic or skeptical thinking will lead them to covertly or overtly challenge standards
- If they have the conceptual, long-range thinking that allows for strategic planning (not everyone can access this talent)
- And most importantly, it will show you the exact challenges they will bring into your business and how to interview them about those performance blocks
- And more…

It will show you HOW a candidate will actually perform on the job. It's an exercise; there are no questions. It cannot be gamed because no one knows what the assessment is asking for or what it will reveal. The items seem completely random and, therefore, people are unable to guess *how* they should answer.

And best of all, it's a universal process. With behavior, if you studied people in the United States and then you went to Japan, you would have to start over because the Japanese culture and behavioral expectations are different.

But the way people think and make decisions is the same everywhere in the world. There is a single process with which the brain works and makes decisions. Each person uses the process, but everyone uses it differently – like a fingerprint. And this assessment objectively and mathematically measures how people make decisions.

This is the only assessment of its kind. It has taken the intangible of thought and made it tangible. It measures performance and not psychological traits.

Nothing is better at predicting, not only *will* a candidate do the job, but will they do it in *your* culture.

I know, at first glance this might seem a little unbelievable and impossible – but imagine, if you could know these things BEFORE you hired someone?

What if you could know the exact questions to ask in order to probe deeper into questionable areas to determine if your candidate WILL be able to do the job for YOU?

For instance, how valuable would it be if you knew that a candidate had a risk of communication problems when it involved customer service? Further, what if you had a list of interview questions specific to that challenge so you could address this problem in the interview?

For example, here are interview questions and notes related to a specific risk related to customer service:

- Suggest an example that illustrates a conflict between themselves and a customer. Test how quickly and how willingly they criticize the customer's point of view. You could say, "Tell me about a time when you had an irate customer calling in asking an irrational question or wanting you to do something crazy"

- Ask them to describe the customer call and then probe into how they assessed the problem. Did they evaluate other alternatives, and what was their recommendation? Stop them frequently and aggressively challenge their ideas. Test their ability to deal with your opposing points of view without becoming too competitive and critical.

Here's another example. In this case, the Hiring MRI performance assessment reveals that your candidate has a tendency to be skeptical about rules, order, structure, and authority. Here is a list of interview questions specific to this challenge:

- Use an example that illustrates biases toward customers. Test them to find how readily they are willing to agree with the negative impression of customers. For instance, "How would you handle calls from patients who don't understand their dental insurance and are upset that their insurance didn't cover the entire procedure?"

- Make statements that are inconsistent, possibly even contradictory. See whether they spot your incorrect thinking.

- Use the follow-up questions and situations below;

  o Describe a situation in which you know that some of your employees are cutting corners to meet schedules and others are looking the other way when coworkers steal things. What would you do?
    - Say nothing and do your job?
    - Speak to your employees and let them know that you think they are hurting the team?

  o What are the steps that you would use to motivate your subordinates to do a better job?

  o What do you think you need to do to improve as a manager?

> o Describe a time when your superiors made a decision that you disagreed with. How did you respond?
>
> o Describe how you would respond to your superiors in the following situation: Your team is one of the most productive groups in the company, but you have the highest percentage of quality control issues. Your superiors reprimand you for the lack of quality control.
>
> o Why did you leave your last job or why are you leaving your current position?
>
> • If your superiors are contacted, what would they say are your best and your worst qualities?

It's an amazing experience to ask a job candidate questions that relate specifically to their own performance challenges.

You will likely see them become uncomfortable or squirm in their chair and to some degree reveal their issue. I've seen candidates countenance change right before my eyes when asked questions from the Hiring MRI Interview Guide.

Candidates will even ask you, "How did you know that about me?" All this from just one, or a few, interview questions targeted directly at their personal performance challenges.

Whatever the red flags might be, the Hiring MRI Performance Assessment has you covered.

When you use the Performance Assessment as the last step in your Hiring MRI formula, I guarantee that you will no longer be blindsided by employees who appear one way in an interview and three months into the job, perform totally differently.

The Hiring MRI Performance Assessment has provided potential employers with insights like...

Prioritized Development Comments

Attitude Toward Authority: (Job-Related Attitudes) -Real Risk

They will likely do things their way regardless of what they tell you or regardless of the consequences. Make certain that you can live with their challenges to your way of thinking and that you can accept their way of doing things.

Sensitivity to Others: (Working with Others) -Real Risk

Describe members of your organization who would be coworkers. Talk in a critical manner which would give them an opportunity to join in your criticism. Test their ability and willingness to be fair in their attitudes.

Prioritized Development Comments

Willing to Follow Directions: (Job-Related Attitudes) -Real Risk

Their insistence on doing things their way can conflict with your need for them to see and accept your way of doing things. Give them directions for solving a problem and test their willingness to try things your way.

Proactive, Conceptual Thinking: (Knowing What to Do) -Real Risk

Their individualism and passion for being inventive and different can lead them to resist tried and proven methods of solving problems. Test their willingness to be patient and to keep their focus on the consequences of their ideas.

Attitude Toward Others: (Working with Others) -Real Risk

Examine their tendency to focus on what is wrong with others. Give them an example of a dispute between themselves and another employee. Ask them to evaluate the perspectives of both parties.

Results Oriented: (Ability to Get Things Done) -Real Risk

Place these individuals in a real-time situation from your work environment to test their ability to see what needs to be done, to respond under pressure and get things done regardless of what is happening around them.

Prioritized Core Strengths

1) Persistence: (Getting Things Done) -Excellent Potential

Strong personal commitment to stay on track and complete goals and tasks regardless of what happens.

2) Seeing Potential Problems: (Managing Problems) -Excellent Potential

Excellent capacity for identifying crucial issues in complex and confusing situations.

3) Insight Into Others: (Managing Others) -Excellent Potential

Keen insight into others combined with a positive attitude builds a realistically optimistic evaluation of others.

4) Intuitive Insight: (Managing Problems) -Excellent Potential

Very good ability for relying on intuitive insight and inner 'gut' feelings for identifying and solving problems.

5) Concrete Organization: (Planning And Organizing) -Excellent Potential

The ability and the willingness to spend time and energy concretely organizing and planning.

But it's not all bad ... the Performance Assessment has also reassured employers that their potential employee would be...

---

6) Using Common Sense: (Managing Problems) -Excellent Potential

Excellent ability to see and understand how to get things done in a practical, commonsense way.

7) Short-Range Planning: (Planning And Organizing) -Excellent Potential

Tendency toward being an idealistic and perfectionistic thinker and planner who tries to plan for every eventuality.

8) Listening To Others: (Managing Others) -Excellent Potential

Ability and willingness to pay attention to the unique viewpoints of others, to their needs and concerns.

9) Flexibility/Adaptability: (Managing Self) -Very Good Potential

Strong personal commitment to what they believe is right combined with the ability to redirect energy when necessary.

So how do you access the Performance Assessments?

If you are like most people, I am guessing that you LOVE what you have read here, you believe that if you could know this information, and more, about potential hires (or even your current employees) it would be beyond beneficial.

Since you're read this book, I want to give you my Hiring MRI Risk-Free Offer. Here's how that works. You can have one of your key employees (someone who you know well – but whom I don't know) take this 15-min exercise. Then jump on the phone with us for a 30-min debrief, and if in that call I don't reveal something I couldn't know about your key employee, then not only will I give you your money back, I will also donate an additional $100 to the charity of your choice.

Go to www.TryRealTalent.com for this Risk-Free opportunity.

JAY HENDERSON'S

Real Talent Hiring

RISK FREE TRIAL OFFER

EXPERIENCE THE HIRING MRI PERFORMANCE ASSESSMENT
AND GET A LIVE REPORT REVIEW

$97

TO GET STARTED, VISIT WWW.TRYREALTALENT.COM

IF YOU BELIEVE WE WASTED YOUR TIME - YOU PAY NOTHING!

CHAPTER 12

HELP! My Key Employee Just Left and I Only Have 2 Weeks...

"I know I'm supposed to hire slow, I know I'm supposed to create my super-star profile and create my super-star magnet, but my key employee just left. What am I supposed to do?"

Okay I know that there are times where you just can't follow the process to a tee, and there are still a few things that you can do to ensure that you do not make a rash decision or hire the wrong person for your job.

You can start by running your ad – but at least start by raising your standards based on what you have learned here. Try and follow the process the best you can; have multiple interviews (don't hire on gut instincts alone).

I like to suggest a trial hire or temporary hire in these situations. You need someone in the job immediately but perhaps you can bring someone on for a short, temporary basis where both of you can determine if this is indeed a good fit. You will need to pay the person a competitive wage for their time, but they will not be hired on full-time to start.

This will allow you to extend your time out to see if you like them and follow the full Hiring MRI formula. While they are there, you must measure their performance; otherwise, the trial hire period does you no good.

This allows you to have a body in the business taking on some of the responsibilities, but you don't have to make your hiring decision today.

But I wouldn't bring someone in for a trial position or temporary hire unless they have completed the Performance Assessment! It's too difficult to invite them to leave after they've been there a while...

Final thoughts… Hopefully by reading this book you have raised your hiring standards.

One of your key jobs is to gather as much information about your candidate as you possibly can and remove all emotion.

Get multiple people from your team involved, but don't let them bulldoze you into making a hiring decision.

Get your key criteria for the position clear – use the super-star profile from chapter 7.

Rather than psyching yourself into hiring someone because you want out of the process, start with the mind-set that a candidate cannot work in your business and affect your life unless they prove to you to be absolutely stellar. Push them about WHY this is the job / business / location for them to spend the next years engaged and performing at a high level.

Remember the 3 Ps. First, protect your business and life. Second, access potential of each team member. Finally, focus on driving performance and grow! Happy hunting.

ABOUT THE AUTHOR

Jay Henderson is the founder of Real Talent Hiring, a unique hiring and management development service for small businesses who want to know exactly who to hire, what to expect, will they succeed, why, what motivates them, and what will they be like in your environment.

Prior to starting Real Talent Hiring, Jay spent 5 years at Stephen R. Covey's company, the Covey Leadership Center. He was a Regional Manager over 9 Central States in the U.S. teaching clients the well-known First Things First program based on Covey's book of the same title. Stephen R. Covey is also author of 7 Habits of Highly Effective People and Principle Centered Leadership. Jay benefited from being trained and certified in all of Stephen's programs.

Jay lives in Raleigh, North Carolina with his wife and children.

JAY HENDERSON'S

Real Talent Hiring

RISK FREE TRIAL OFFER

EXPERIENCE THE HIRING MRI PERFORMANCE ASSESSMENT
AND GET A LIVE REPORT REVIEW

$97

TO GET STARTED, VISIT WWW.TRYREALTALENT.COM

IF YOU BELIEVE WE WASTED YOUR TIME - YOU PAY NOTHING!